THE
WHITE
CRAYON

Finding the beauty in the unseen

BLUEROSE PUBLISHERS
U.K.

Copyright © Mayyuri Srivastava 2024

All rights reserved by author. No part of this publication may be reproduced, stored in a retrieval system or transmitted in any form or by any means, electronic, mechanical, photocopying, recording or otherwise, without the prior permission of the author. Although every precaution has been taken to verify the accuracy of the information contained herein, the publisher assumes no responsibility for any errors or omissions. No liability is assumed for damages that may result from the use of information contained within.

BlueRose Publishers takes no responsibility for any damages, losses, or liabilities that may arise from the use or misuse of the information, products, or services provided in this publication.

For permissions requests or inquiries regarding this publication, please contact:

BLUEROSE PUBLISHERS
www.BlueRoseONE.com
info@bluerosepublishers.com
+4407342408967

ISBN: 978-93-6783-390-2

Cover design: Daksh
Typesetting: Tanya Raj Upadhyay

First Edition: November 2024

"Dedicated to my Grandmother and Mother"

&

"All those who feel insecure in the unseen"

PREFACE

In a world that moves at an ever-accelerating pace, it is easy to become caught in the blur of the obvious—the loud, the bright, and the bold, which demand our attention and dominate our lives. But beneath this surface, there exists a deeper, quieter reality. It is a world of subtleties, of details that often go unnoticed, of moments and elements that, when observed and appreciated, reveal a beauty more profound than what meets the eye.

This book is an invitation to slow down and seek the beauty that lies in the unseen—the overlooked corners of life, the fleeting moments between heartbeats, and the quiet spaces where wonder resides. It is about finding grace in the shadows, meaning in the mundane, and poetry in the stillness. We so often overlook these treasures in our pursuit of the obvious and the spectacular, but it is in the seemingly insignificant that we may discover our most meaningful truths.

Throughout these pages, I share stories, reflections, and observations that seek to unveil the beauty that surrounds us—hidden in plain sight, waiting to be found. It is not a beauty defined by society's standards or shaped by convention, but one that emerges through attentiveness and a shift in perspective. I hope that as you journey through these reflections, you, too, will come to see the world differently and discover the richness of what lies beneath the surface.

May this book encourage you to look again—to seek with your heart as much as with your eyes—and to find beauty where it is least expected. The unseen is not invisible; it is simply waiting to be seen.

Let us begin.

TABLE OF CONTENTS

Chapter 1: Feeling Invisible: The Beginning of the Journey 1

Chapter 2: Understanding the Power of Subtlety 9

Chapter 3: Finding Purpose in the Shadows 18

Chapter 4: Embracing Uniqueness and Diversity 24

Chapter 5: The Importance of Subtlety and Nuance 32

Chapter 6: The Power of Patience and Persistence .. 38

Chapter 7: The Beauty of Diversity and Collaboration 45

Chapter 8: The Quiet Triumph of Self-Acceptance .. 52

CHAPTER I:
FEELING INVISIBLE: THE BEGINNING OF THE JOURNEY

The feeling of being invisible is universal. Whether we are young or old, in the midst of a bustling city or in the quiet corners of our homes, every one of us has experienced moments where we feel unnoticed or unimportant. It can happen at school when we raise our hands and no one calls on us, at work when our ideas are overlooked, or even at home when our efforts seem to go unappreciated. These moments of invisibility can leave us feeling disconnected, unsure of our value, and questioning our place in the world.

Much like the white crayon in a box full of vibrant colors, we wonder: *What is my purpose?* When everyone around us seems to shine so brightly, it's easy to feel as though we don't belong. We start to believe that if we aren't standing out or making a visible impact, we must not matter. But the truth is that feeling invisible is often just the beginning of a profound journey — one that leads us to discover our unique value and purpose.

The Loneliness of Feeling Unseen

Loneliness is perhaps the most immediate and painful emotion associated with invisibility. There's a distinct kind of loneliness that comes from being surrounded by people but feeling as though no one truly sees you. It's a feeling that can sneak up on us in the most unexpected places: in the classroom, at a family gathering, or even in the company of friends.

Imagine the white crayon in the box. It sits among all the other crayons, watching as the red, blue, yellow, and green crayons are chosen time and time again. They create bold strokes, vibrant shapes, and eye-catching designs. Meanwhile, the white crayon waits, unsure if it will ever be picked up, let alone used. It's there, but it might as well not be. This metaphor captures the essence of what it feels like to be in a group yet feel completely unnoticed — present, but invisible.

This loneliness can lead to self-doubt. We start to wonder: *Is there something wrong with me? Am I doing something wrong? Why can't others see my value?* These thoughts, if left unchecked, can snowball into feelings of unworthiness and low self-esteem. It's natural to want to feel seen and validated by others, and when that doesn't happen, we question our own significance.

For some, these feelings of invisibility start early in life. Children who don't fit into the obvious categories of the loud, outgoing, or athletic may feel like they're on the sidelines. They may struggle to find their place in social circles or feel overshadowed by siblings who receive more attention. As adults, these feelings can continue in different forms: being overlooked for a promotion at work, not being invited to social events, or feeling like the efforts we put into our relationships go unrecognized.

The Paradox of the Quiet Contributor

In a world that celebrates boldness and visibility, we are often taught that the louder we are, the more valuable we become. Success, we are told, belongs to those who stand out, who command attention, and who make a splash. But not everyone fits into this mold. Some of us are quiet contributors, adding value in ways that aren't always immediately obvious. Just because our contributions aren't as flashy doesn't mean they are any less important.

The white crayon represents this paradox perfectly. It may not create bold, vibrant strokes on its own, but it plays an essential role in the bigger picture. It's the crayon that adds highlights to the picture, brings contrast to the darker shades, and gives dimension to the drawing. Without the white crayon, the colors on the page would blend together, losing their definition and clarity.

In real life, quiet contributors are often the ones who keep things running smoothly behind the scenes. They're the coworkers who stay late to finish a project without seeking credit, the family members who take care of small but essential tasks that go unnoticed, and the friends who provide a listening ear when others need support. Their impact may not be obvious at first glance, but without them, the picture would be incomplete.

The struggle for quiet contributors is that because their contributions are subtle, they can often go unrecognized — and that can be disheartening. We live in a world that rewards visibility, and when our efforts don't receive the acknowledgment we feel they deserve, it's easy to start believing that they don't matter at all. But this belief couldn't be further from the truth.

The challenge for quiet contributors, much like the white crayon, is learning to recognize and appreciate their own value, even when others don't. It's about understanding that not every contribution needs to be loud or attention-grabbing to be meaningful. Sometimes, it's the quiet, consistent efforts that make the biggest difference in the long run.

The Emotional Impact of Being Overlooked

Feeling invisible doesn't just affect how we see ourselves — it can also take a toll on our emotions. When we feel unseen or unappreciated, it's natural to feel sad, frustrated, or even angry. We might start to withdraw from others, thinking, *If they don't see me, why should I bother trying to connect?* These feelings of disconnection can lead to isolation, which only deepens the sense of loneliness.

For the white crayon, watching the other colors being used over and over again can stir up feelings of sadness and jealousy. It wonders, *Why can't I be like them? Why am I always left behind?* This is a feeling many of us can relate to — the sense that no matter how hard we try, we can't seem to fit into the roles that others occupy so easily. We start to believe that there's something wrong with us, that we're flawed in some way, and that's why we're not being noticed.

But the truth is, there's nothing wrong with being different. Just because we don't fit into the obvious roles doesn't mean we don't have a role to play. The challenge is shifting our perspective and learning to see our unique contributions as valuable, even if they don't look like everyone else's.

Empathy plays a key role in overcoming the emotional impact of being overlooked. When we start to recognize that everyone has moments of feeling invisible, it becomes easier to connect with others and understand their struggles. We begin to see that we're not alone in our feelings, and that in itself can be incredibly healing.

Turning Invisibility Into a Strength

Feeling invisible doesn't have to be a negative experience. In fact, it can be a powerful opportunity for growth and self-reflection. When we feel unseen, we are given the chance to look inward and ask ourselves some important questions: *What truly matters to me? What are my strengths? How can I contribute to the world in a way that feels authentic to me?*

The white crayon's journey of invisibility is also a journey of self-discovery. At first, it feels disheartened by its perceived lack of value. But as it spends time observing the other colors and reflecting on its own unique qualities, it starts to see itself in a new light. It realizes that while it may not add bold colors to the page, it can bring something just as important: balance, contrast, and subtle beauty. Without the white crayon, the picture would be incomplete.

For those of us who feel invisible, this chapter of life is an opportunity to discover our own hidden strengths. It's a time to explore what makes us unique and how we can use those qualities to make a positive impact in the world. Rather than trying to fit into someone else's mold, we can start to embrace our individuality and find fulfillment in our own journey.

The Road to Self-Acceptance

Self-acceptance is one of the most powerful tools we have for overcoming feelings of invisibility. When we accept ourselves — flaws, strengths, and all — we stop seeking validation from others and start finding it within ourselves. This doesn't mean we don't want to be seen or appreciated by others, but it means that our sense of worth is no longer dependent on external recognition.

For the white crayon, self-acceptance comes when it realizes that its value isn't determined by how often it's used or how visible its contributions are. Its worth comes from the unique role it plays in the bigger picture. It understands that it doesn't need to compete with the other colors, because its purpose is different from theirs. And that's okay.

Self-acceptance is a journey, not a destination. It's something we have to work on every day, especially when we live in a world that constantly pushes us to compare ourselves to others. But when we start to accept and embrace our own uniqueness, we free ourselves from the need to be seen in a specific way. We can start to appreciate the quiet, subtle contributions we make to the world, knowing that they are just as important as the bold, visible ones.

A New Perspective on Invisibility

By the end of this chapter, we come to understand that invisibility isn't inherently a bad thing. In fact, it can be a source of strength, growth, and self-discovery. Just like the white crayon, we may not always stand out in obvious ways, but our contributions are still essential to the bigger picture.

This chapter invites readers to embrace their feelings of invisibility as an opportunity to learn more about themselves. It encourages them to find value in their own unique qualities, even when those qualities aren't immediately recognized by others. And most importantly, it reminds us that just because we feel invisible doesn't mean we are invisible. We all have a role to play in the masterpiece of life — and that role is just as important as any other.

In the next chapter, we will explore the power of subtlety and how even the quietest contributions can make a profound impact on the world. But for now, let's sit with the knowledge that invisibility is not the end of the story. It's just the beginning.

CHAPTER 2:
UNDERSTANDING THE POWER OF SUBTLETY

In a world that often celebrates the loudest voices and the brightest stars, subtlety can be misunderstood and undervalued. We are conditioned to believe that success and recognition come only to those who make the biggest impact, the boldest statements, and the most visible changes. But there is immense power in subtlety — the kind that quietly shapes our experiences, influences our lives, and often goes unnoticed until we step back and see the whole picture.

The white crayon's journey is one of subtlety. At first, it feels overlooked, questioning whether its contributions matter in a world filled with vivid colors. But as it begins to understand its role, the white crayon realizes that subtlety can have a profound impact. It may not dominate the page with bold strokes, but its soft, delicate touches bring balance, contrast, and depth to the artwork. Without those quiet contributions, the picture would lack dimension and clarity.

This chapter explores the quiet strength that comes from subtlety, teaching us to appreciate the understated contributions we make and the often unseen ways we influence the world around us.

The Misunderstanding of Subtlety

Subtlety is often confused with insignificance. If something isn't immediately obvious or attention-grabbing, it can be easy to dismiss it as unimportant. This is especially true in a culture that glorifies extroversion, bold leadership, and loud achievements. We are taught to believe that in order to make a difference, we have to be seen, heard, and celebrated. But this belief overlooks the incredible power of subtlety.

Think of the white crayon. When we first look at a box of crayons, our eyes are naturally drawn to the brightest colors: reds, blues, greens, and yellows. The white crayon sits quietly in the box, often overlooked because it doesn't make the same visual impact. On a blank white page, it can seem nearly invisible. But when used thoughtfully, the white crayon transforms the picture. It highlights, creates contrast, and gives depth to the other colors, making them stand out even more.

In life, subtlety works in much the same way. There are people whose contributions are quiet but essential. They may not be the ones standing in the spotlight, but their efforts create the foundation that allows others to shine. These are the people who offer support behind the scenes, who listen more than they speak, and who provide the small but vital details that complete the picture. They may not always be recognized, but without them, the world would lack balance.

This chapter challenges the reader to rethink their definition of success and value. It invites us to see the importance of subtlety in our own lives and in the lives of those around us. Just because something isn't obvious doesn't mean it isn't impactful.

The Quiet Contributors

Quiet contributors are the people who work diligently in the background, often without seeking recognition or praise. They are the ones who ensure that things run smoothly, who provide emotional support, and who offer small acts of kindness that make a big difference. Their contributions may not be celebrated in the same way as more visible achievements, but they are no less important.

Consider a classroom setting. There are always students who speak up frequently, who answer questions with confidence, and who take on leadership roles in group projects. These students are often praised for their participation and seen as the most engaged. But what about the quiet students? The ones who may not raise their hands as often, but who listen carefully, work hard, and offer thoughtful contributions in smaller settings? Their presence may be less noticeable, but their learning and growth are just as valuable.

Similarly, in a workplace, there are always employees who take charge, lead meetings, and present ideas with flair. These individuals often receive promotions and accolades for their leadership. But behind every successful project, there are team members whose efforts are just as crucial — the ones who stay late to finish tasks, who support their colleagues, and who ensure that every detail is taken care of. Their contributions may be less visible, but without them, the project would fall apart.

In families, too, there are quiet contributors. These are the people who take on the less glamorous tasks: cooking meals, doing laundry, organizing schedules, and providing emotional support. They may not receive the same level of attention or praise as others, but their efforts are what keep the family functioning smoothly. Without their quiet contributions, the family would struggle to maintain balance.

The Power of Nuance in Relationships

Subtlety plays a crucial role in relationships, whether romantic, familial, or platonic. In a world that often values grand gestures — extravagant gifts, public declarations of love, and bold expressions of affection — it's easy to overlook the quiet ways in which we connect with others. But it is often these small, nuanced actions that build the strongest and most lasting relationships.

The white crayon's role in a drawing can be likened to the quiet acts of care that strengthen relationships over time. Just as the white crayon adds highlights and depth to a picture, subtle gestures of love and support add depth to our connections with others. These might be things like remembering a small detail from a conversation, offering a kind word when someone is feeling down, or simply being present when a friend or family member needs us.

In romantic relationships, for example, it's easy to get caught up in the idea that love must be expressed in big, dramatic ways. But the reality is that lasting love is often built on the foundation of small, everyday acts of care and consideration. It's in the thoughtful text message, the quiet support during difficult times, and the shared moments of laughter that real intimacy is formed. These subtle acts may not always be noticed or celebrated, but they are the glue that holds relationships together.

In friendships, too, the power of subtlety cannot be overstated. True friendship is not about constant activity or dramatic displays of loyalty; it's about the quiet moments of understanding and connection. A friend who listens without judgment, who offers support without fanfare, and who is simply there when needed is often the most valuable kind of friend. Their subtle presence may not always be obvious, but it is deeply felt.

This chapter encourages readers to recognize and appreciate the quiet, nuanced ways in which we connect with others. It reminds us that while grand gestures can be meaningful, it is often the small, everyday acts of kindness and support that create the strongest bonds.

Recognizing Our Own Subtle Contributions

One of the greatest challenges for those who operate in subtle ways is recognizing their own value. When we aren't the loudest or the most visible, it can be easy to fall into the trap of thinking that our contributions don't matter. This is especially true in environments that prioritize extroversion and boldness. But just because our efforts aren't immediately recognized doesn't mean they aren't important.

The white crayon, for much of its journey, struggles with this very issue. It watches the other colors being chosen again and again, and it wonders if it has any value at all. But over time, the white crayon begins to see how its subtle touches transform the picture. It adds light to the dark areas, creates soft edges, and brings out the beauty in the other colors. Its contribution, though subtle, is essential.

In our own lives, it's important to take time to reflect on the ways in which we make a difference, even if those differences aren't immediately visible. Perhaps we're the ones who keep the peace in a family, who offer quiet support to colleagues, or who provide a calming presence in a stressful situation. These contributions may not always be recognized or celebrated, but they are valuable nonetheless.

One way to start recognizing our own subtle contributions is by keeping track of the small ways in which we add value to the lives of others. This could be through journaling or simply taking a few moments at the end of each day to reflect on the quiet ways we've made a difference. By doing this, we begin to see that our contributions are meaningful, even if they aren't always acknowledged by others.

Celebrating the Power of Subtlety

While subtle contributions are often overlooked in a culture that prioritizes visibility, it's important to celebrate the power of subtlety. This chapter invites readers to not only recognize their own subtle contributions but to appreciate the quiet efforts of those around them. When we start to see the beauty in subtlety, we begin to understand that not every impact needs to be loud or dramatic to be profound.

Just as the white crayon brings depth and balance to a picture, subtle actions bring richness and meaning to our lives. It's the soft touch that highlights the beauty in the bolder strokes, the quiet moments that give contrast to the noise, and the gentle presence that provides balance in a chaotic world. Without subtlety, the picture of life would be incomplete.

The power of subtlety lies in its ability to create change and influence in ways that are often unnoticed but deeply felt. It's the difference between a picture that is flat and one that has depth, between a relationship that is surface-level and one that is deeply connected. Subtlety adds layers of meaning and complexity to the world, and it is something to be cherished and celebrated.

Conclusion

In this chapter, we've explored the often-overlooked power of subtlety. We've seen how quiet contributions, though less visible, are no less important than bold actions. Whether in our work, relationships, or daily interactions, subtlety has the ability to create profound and lasting change.

The white crayon's journey is a reminder that we don't have to be the loudest or the most visible to make a difference. Our quiet efforts, our nuanced contributions, and our subtle acts of care are just as valuable. By embracing the power of subtlety, we can find meaning and purpose in the quiet moments, knowing that even the smallest touches can have a lasting impact.

As we move forward, let's take time to appreciate the subtle contributions we make and the quiet ways in which we influence the world around us.

CHAPTER 3:
FINDING PURPOSE IN THE SHADOWS

Purpose is something we all seek at different points in our lives. It gives us direction, meaning, and a sense of belonging in a world that can sometimes feel chaotic. Yet, for those of us who feel invisible or overshadowed by others, discovering our purpose can be particularly challenging. We may find ourselves asking, "If I'm not seen or recognized, do I have a purpose? What am I meant to contribute?"

In this chapter, we delve into the white crayon's journey of self-discovery, which reflects the universal struggle of finding purpose in a world that often overlooks subtle contributions. As the white crayon comes to understand, purpose isn't about being the most visible or having the loudest impact. Rather, it's about recognizing the unique role we play, even when that role is more in the background. The journey to finding purpose is not always straightforward, but it is one that each of us must take.

The Search for Meaning

For the white crayon, the journey to find its purpose begins with feelings of doubt and confusion. Surrounded by colors that seem to have obvious roles, the white crayon can't help but question its own place in the box. It watches the reds and blues being chosen to create vibrant landscapes, while it sits untouched, wondering what it can possibly add to the picture. The white crayon's dilemma mirrors our own internal struggles when we feel left out or unsure of our direction in life.

It's easy to fall into the trap of comparing ourselves to others, especially in a world where success is often equated with visibility. If we aren't standing out or making waves, we might assume that we aren't contributing anything meaningful. But purpose is not about being noticed; it's about understanding the unique value we bring to the world, even if it's less obvious.

The white crayon's journey teaches us that finding purpose is an inward exploration. It's about stepping away from external expectations and discovering what truly matters to us. It's about asking ourselves: *What do I enjoy doing? What strengths do I have that others might overlook? How can I contribute in ways that feel authentic to me?*

Embracing the Role of the Quiet Supporter

The white crayon eventually comes to understand that its purpose lies not in adding bold colors to the page, but in complementing the other colors. It may not be chosen to create the most eye-catching parts of the picture, but it brings light to dark spaces, creates subtle details, and helps other colors shine brighter. Without the white crayon, the picture would lack contrast and clarity. Its contributions may be subtle, but they are essential.

This realization reflects the role of the quiet supporter in real life. Not everyone is meant to lead from the front or be the star of the show. Some of us are meant to support others, to create the conditions for success, and to bring out the best in those around us. These roles, though less visible, are just as important as the more prominent ones.

In our daily lives, we might be the ones who provide emotional support to friends and family, who offer encouragement without seeking recognition, or who take care of the small details that make a big difference. We may not receive praise for these actions, but they are critical to the well-being of others and to the overall harmony of our environments.

Embracing the role of the quiet supporter requires a shift in perspective. Instead of seeing ourselves as less valuable because we aren't in the spotlight, we can start to appreciate the ways in which our subtle contributions create balance and wholeness. Just as the white crayon adds depth and contrast to the drawing, we, too, add depth to the lives of those around us.

The Impact of Small, Meaningful Actions

One of the greatest lessons we can learn from the white crayon's journey is the power of small, meaningful actions. Purpose doesn't always come from grand gestures or significant achievements. Sometimes, it's the small, consistent acts of kindness, support, and thoughtfulness that have the greatest impact.

Think about a time when someone did something small for you that made a big difference. It could have been a kind word on a difficult day, a thoughtful gesture when you were feeling down, or simply someone being there when you needed them most. These moments may not have been loud or attention-grabbing, but they left a lasting impression.

The white crayon teaches us that even the smallest contributions can have a ripple effect. A single highlight can bring an entire drawing to life, just as a single act of kindness can brighten someone's day. Purpose is not about the scale of our actions, but the intention behind them. When we act with care, thoughtfulness, and authenticity, even the smallest actions can have a profound impact.

The Freedom of Letting Go of Comparison

A key part of the white crayon's journey to finding purpose is letting go of comparison. Early on, the white crayon feels insecure because it doesn't fit into the same mold as the other colors. It watches the reds, blues, and greens being chosen to create bold, vibrant images and feels inadequate by comparison. This feeling of inadequacy is something many of us can relate to.

Comparison is a natural human tendency, but it can also be one of the biggest obstacles to finding our purpose. When we constantly measure ourselves against others, we lose sight of our own unique strengths and contributions. We start to believe that if we aren't achieving the same things as those around us, we aren't valuable.

The white crayon's turning point comes when it realizes that its purpose is different from the other colors — and that's okay. It doesn't need to compete with the bold colors because its role is complementary. Similarly, in life, we all have different strengths, paths, and purposes. Our value isn't diminished just because we don't fit into someone else's mold.

When we let go of comparison, we free ourselves to discover our true purpose. We stop trying to fit into roles that don't suit us and start embracing the ones that do. Just as the white crayon finds peace in its unique role, we, too, can find fulfillment when we focus on our own path rather than comparing it to others.

Finding Peace in Our Purpose

Ultimately, finding purpose is about more than just understanding our role in the world. It's about finding peace within ourselves. The white crayon's journey is a reminder that purpose is not something we find by looking outward — it's something we discover by looking inward. It's about recognizing the unique ways in which we contribute, embracing our individuality, and letting go of the need for external validation.

When we find peace in our purpose, we stop chasing after recognition or approval. Instead, we find fulfillment in knowing that we are making a difference, even if it's in subtle, quiet ways. Just as the white crayon learns to appreciate its role in the bigger picture, we can learn to appreciate the ways in which we add value to the world, even if our contributions aren't always visible to others.

Finding purpose is a journey that takes time, patience, and self-reflection. But when we embrace our unique path and recognize the power of our subtle contributions, we begin to see that we are not invisible. We are essential.

In the next chapter, we will explore how embracing our individuality and uniqueness can lead to a deeper sense of connection with ourselves and others. But for now, let's sit with the knowledge that our purpose, though sometimes subtle, is always significant.

CHAPTER 4:
EMBRACING UNIQUENESS AND DIVERSITY

As the white crayon continues its journey, it begins to understand something powerful: being different is not a weakness but a strength. In a world where we often feel the pressure to fit in or conform to certain norms, embracing our uniqueness and recognizing the value of diversity can be transformative. This chapter explores the beauty of individuality and the important role diversity plays in creating a more vibrant and balanced world.

Just like the white crayon, we all have something unique to contribute. Whether our differences are subtle or bold, they add to the richness of life's experiences. The key to unlocking our potential and finding fulfillment lies in accepting, celebrating, and embracing the very things that set us apart. Through this journey, the white crayon teaches us that true strength comes from understanding and valuing what makes us unique, and seeing how our differences complement the world around us.

The Pressure to Conform

In many ways, the white crayon's initial struggle is one that we all face at some point in our lives: the pressure to conform. From a young age, we are often taught that fitting in is the key to success and acceptance. Whether it's following societal expectations, adhering to cultural norms, or conforming to peer pressure, the message is clear: to be like everyone else is to be accepted, and to stand out is to risk rejection.

The white crayon experiences this pressure within its own crayon box. It looks around and sees the bright colors being used over and over again to create beautiful, vivid images. Meanwhile, it sits untouched, feeling as though it has no place in the world of art because it doesn't add the same kind of bold, obvious color. In its mind, if it could just be like the other crayons — if it could be red, blue, or green — then it would be chosen more often and have a greater sense of purpose.

But the white crayon's dilemma reflects a broader truth: when we feel different, we often question our worth. We may think that if we could just blend in more, conform to the expectations of others, or change who we are, we would be more accepted and valued. But the white crayon's journey teaches us that trying to be like everyone else only diminishes our uniqueness, which is the very thing that makes us valuable.

The Beauty of Individuality

As the white crayon begins to reflect on its role in the world of colors, it comes to an important realization: its uniqueness is not a limitation but a strength. While it may not add bold colors to the page, it has the ability to bring light, contrast, and subtlety to a drawing. Without the white crayon, the other colors would lack balance and dimension. The white crayon enhances their beauty by offering something different — something that no other color can provide.

This realization is a powerful metaphor for individuality in our own lives. Each of us brings something unique to the table, whether it's a different perspective, a specific skill set, or a personality trait that sets us apart. These differences are not things to be hidden or changed; they are what make us valuable. Just as the white crayon enhances the other colors by being true to itself, we, too, enhance the world around us by embracing our individuality.

In a world that often values sameness and conformity, it's important to remember that true innovation, creativity, and progress come from diversity. When we embrace our unique qualities, we not only bring out the best in ourselves but also contribute to a richer, more vibrant world. Our differences are what allow us to see things from new angles, solve problems in creative ways, and connect with others in meaningful ways.

The Role of Diversity in Creating Balance

The white crayon's journey also highlights the essential role that diversity plays in creating balance and harmony. In a box of crayons, no single color is more important than the others. Each one has its own role to play, and together, they create a more complete picture. The same is true in life: diversity is what brings balance, depth, and richness to our experiences.

Imagine a world where everyone was the same — where we all thought the same way, had the same talents, and approached life in the same manner. It would be a world lacking in creativity, innovation, and growth. Just as a drawing made with only one color would be flat and uninteresting, a world without diversity would be dull and limited.

Diversity allows us to see the world from multiple perspectives, to learn from one another, and to grow in ways that we couldn't on our own. It's through our differences that we gain new insights, challenge our assumptions, and develop a deeper understanding of the world around us. Just as the white crayon brings light and contrast to the page, diversity brings light and contrast to our lives, helping us appreciate the full spectrum of human experiences.

Embracing and Celebrating Differences

One of the most important lessons the white crayon learns on its journey is the value of celebrating differences rather than fearing or rejecting them. At the beginning of the story, the white crayon feels isolated and insecure because it doesn't fit in with the other colors. It views its differences as weaknesses and believes that being different makes it less valuable. But over time, it begins to see that its uniqueness is not something to hide, but something to celebrate.

In our own lives, it can be easy to fall into the trap of viewing our differences as flaws. We may worry that standing out will make us vulnerable to judgment or rejection, and so we try to downplay or hide the things that make us unique. But the white crayon's story reminds us that our differences are what make us special. When we embrace and celebrate those differences, we not only become more confident in ourselves but also help create a more inclusive and accepting world.

Celebrating diversity doesn't mean simply tolerating differences; it means actively appreciating and valuing them. It means recognizing that every individual brings something important to the table and that our differences are what make us stronger as a whole. Whether it's in the workplace, in our communities, or in our personal relationships, embracing and celebrating diversity leads to greater understanding, empathy, and connection.

The Intersection of Uniqueness and Community

While the white crayon's journey is one of self-discovery, it also emphasizes the importance of community. The white crayon doesn't find its purpose in isolation; it finds it in relation to the other colors. Its role is not to stand alone but to complement and enhance the other crayons. This speaks to a larger truth about individuality and community: our uniqueness is most powerful when it is shared with others.

In our own lives, we are not meant to exist in isolation. While it's important to embrace our individuality, it's equally important to recognize how our unique qualities contribute to the larger community. When we bring our authentic selves to the table, we enrich the experiences of those around us. Just as the white crayon adds depth and balance to a drawing, we, too, add value to our communities by sharing our unique perspectives, talents, and ideas.

At the same time, community plays an important role in helping us embrace our individuality. When we are surrounded by people who appreciate and celebrate our differences, we feel more confident in being ourselves. A supportive community allows us to grow into our full potential and encourages us to use our unique gifts to make a positive impact.

Moving from Acceptance to Empowerment

The white crayon's journey from feeling invisible to understanding its value reflects a broader shift from acceptance to empowerment. At first, the white crayon simply wants to be accepted — to feel like it belongs in the box with the other crayons. But as it comes to embrace its unique role, it moves beyond acceptance and begins to feel empowered by its differences. It realizes that its contributions are essential, and it takes pride in the role it plays.

This shift from acceptance to empowerment is something we can all experience when we embrace our uniqueness. It's one thing to accept that we are different; it's another to feel empowered by those differences. When we move from a mindset of simply wanting to fit in to one of celebrating and owning our individuality, we unlock our full potential.

Empowerment comes from recognizing that our differences are strengths, not weaknesses. It comes from understanding that we have something valuable to contribute, even if it doesn't look the same as what others are contributing. And it comes from feeling confident in who we are, knowing that our uniqueness adds richness to the world around us.

Conclusion: Uniqueness as a Source of Strength

In this chapter, we've explored the white crayon's journey to embracing its uniqueness and the important role that diversity plays in creating balance and harmony. The white crayon's story teaches us that being different is not something to fear or hide but something to celebrate. Our differences are what make us valuable, and when we embrace them, we unlock our full potential.

As we move forward, let's take the time to reflect on our own uniqueness and the ways in which we can celebrate and embrace the diversity of those around us. By doing so, we create a world that is not only more inclusive but also more vibrant and full of possibility. Just as the white crayon brings light and depth to a drawing, our uniqueness brings light and depth to the world.

CHAPTER 5:
THE IMPORTANCE OF SUBTLETY AND NUANCE

In the loud and fast-paced world we live in, subtlety and nuance are often overlooked. Boldness, speed, and directness are celebrated, while the quieter, more understated elements can fade into the background. However, much like the white crayon in our story, subtle contributions can be powerful, adding depth and balance to the bigger picture. They offer a quiet strength that sustains and enhances the world around them. In this chapter, we will explore how the white crayon's journey helps us appreciate the role of subtlety and nuance in our lives. We'll look at how these qualities contribute to meaningful interactions, decision-making, and self-awareness. Just as the white crayon brings light to darker areas in a drawing, subtlety and nuance can bring clarity and perspective to our lives in ways that louder, more obvious approaches often miss.

Subtlety in a World of Boldness The world often values what is big and bold. In a box of crayons, bright colors like red, blue, and yellow are typically chosen first, and it's easy to see why: they make an immediate impact. These colors demand attention and are used to create bold, eye-catching images. In contrast, the white crayon is often left behind, as its contribution is less obvious. This can be likened to how we view boldness in real life. We often praise loud ideas, strong opinions, and assertive actions. People who speak up and stand out are seen as leaders, while those who take a quieter, more reflective approach can be overlooked. Yet, just like the white crayon, subtle contributions often play a crucial role behind the scenes. Without the white crayon, drawings would lack contrast, clarity, and balance. Its presence is felt, even if it's not always seen. In our lives, subtlety can take many forms: a quiet word of encouragement, a thoughtful gesture, or the careful consideration of different perspectives before making a decision. These small actions might not garner attention, but they are often the ones that have the most lasting impact.

The Power of Nuance in Relationships Nuance is what makes relationships rich and complex. It's the delicate balance between saying too much and saying too little, between giving advice and simply listening, between expressing our feelings and holding space for the feelings of others. Just as the white crayon adds subtle highlights that bring depth to a drawing, nuance in communication and behavior adds layers of understanding and connection to our relationships. For example, think about a time when someone gave you exactly the right words of comfort in a difficult situation. They didn't overwhelm you with advice or try to solve your problem immediately. Instead, they offered a quiet, thoughtful response that showed they truly understood what you were going through. This is the power of nuance. It allows us to be present in the moment, to respond thoughtfully rather than react impulsively, and to build deeper, more meaningful connections with others. The white crayon's journey reminds us that not everything needs to be said or done with boldness. Sometimes, it's the quiet moments, the subtle gestures, and the nuanced responses that make all the difference in how we connect with others.

Finding Strength in Subtlety Subtlety is often mistaken for weakness. In a world that encourages us to be loud and assertive, being subtle can feel like we're holding back or not expressing ourselves fully. But the white crayon shows us that subtlety is not about being passive or weak; it's about using our strength in a more thoughtful, measured way. In the story, the white crayon doesn't add vibrant splashes of color, but it brings something equally important: light and clarity. It highlights edges, brightens areas that would otherwise be too dark, and creates balance in the drawing. Without it, the image would be incomplete. Similarly, in our own lives, subtle actions can be just as powerful as bold ones. Whether it's quietly leading by example, offering support without fanfare, or making decisions based on careful consideration rather than impulsiveness, subtlety is a strength that can guide us through life's complexities. In fact, subtlety often requires more strength than boldness. It takes self-awareness to recognize when to hold back and when to step forward. It takes patience to listen and observe before acting. And it takes confidence to trust that our quiet contributions are just as valuable as more visible ones.

Subtle Contributions in Everyday Life Subtlety and nuance show up in many aspects of our daily lives, often without us realizing it. They influence how we interact with others, how we make decisions, and how we navigate challenges. Let's explore a few areas where these qualities play a crucial role: 1. Communication: In conversations, the way we listen is just as important as the way we speak. Listening with nuance means paying attention not just to the words being said, but also to the tone, body language, and emotions behind them. It's about reading between the lines and responding in a way that shows empathy and understanding. 2. Problem-solving: When faced with a challenge, bold solutions can be effective, but they are not always the best approach. Nuance allows us to see the complexity of a situation and consider different angles before acting. It helps us find creative, thoughtful solutions that may not be immediately obvious. 3. Self-reflection: Subtlety plays a key role in self-awareness. It's easy to focus on the big, bold aspects of our personalities, but nuance helps us recognize the smaller, more intricate parts of ourselves — our motivations, our fears, and our inner conflicts. This deeper understanding allows us to grow and make more informed choices in life. 4. Leadership: Effective leaders often lead with nuance. Instead of imposing their ideas or making decisions impulsively, they take the time to listen to their team, weigh different perspectives, and make thoughtful choices. They know when to step back and let others shine, and when to offer subtle guidance and support.

Nuance as a Path to Wisdom One of the most valuable lessons the white crayon teaches us is that subtlety and nuance are pathways to wisdom. Wisdom is not about knowing all the answers or having bold, sweeping ideas. It's about understanding the complexities of life, seeing beyond the surface, and making decisions with care and insight. Just as the white crayon brings subtle highlights that make a drawing come alive, nuance allows us to see the shades of meaning in every situation. It helps us navigate the gray areas of life — the places where there are no clear right or wrong answers, but rather a spectrum of possibilities. By embracing subtlety, we can approach life with a deeper sense of understanding and compassion.

Conclusion: A Quiet, Lasting Impact As we reflect on the white crayon's journey and its role in the larger picture, we are reminded that subtlety and nuance are not to be underestimated. They may not always be the loudest or most visible qualities, but their impact is profound. Just as the white crayon brings balance and clarity to a drawing, subtlety and nuance bring depth and wisdom to our lives. The lesson of this chapter is clear: we don't always have to make a big splash to make a difference. Sometimes, the quietest actions and the most thoughtful gestures have the longest-lasting impact. By embracing subtlety and nuance, we can navigate life with grace, wisdom, and a deeper connection to the world around us.

CHAPTER 6:
THE POWER OF PATIENCE AND PERSISTENCE

In today's fast-paced, result-driven world, the virtues of patience and persistence often go unappreciated. We're constantly bombarded with messages that encourage us to act fast, think on our feet, and get results quickly. Instant gratification has become the norm, making the concepts of waiting, enduring, and persisting through challenges seem almost archaic. But, much like the white crayon's quiet and understated importance, patience and persistence offer a deep and enduring strength that far outlasts fleeting success.

In this chapter, we explore the crucial role patience and persistence play in achieving meaningful progress, the impact they have on personal growth, and how, like the white crayon's subtle contributions, these qualities often work behind the scenes to create something lasting and impactful. Success may not always be immediate or loud, but with patience and persistence, it becomes deeper, more meaningful, and often far more resilient.

The Illusion of Quick Success

We live in a time where instant success stories dominate the narrative. Social media, news outlets, and popular culture tend to highlight the overnight triumphs of individuals or companies, leading many to believe that success should come quickly or not at all. However, these stories often omit the long, difficult road of effort, failure, and perseverance that preceded the final victory. We tend to forget that the white crayon's impact in a drawing, while subtle and often unnoticed at first, is what brings clarity and balance over time.

In real life, true success is rarely instant. Patience and persistence are what carry us through the times when progress seems slow or invisible. Think of a seed buried beneath the soil. For days, weeks, or even months, nothing appears to be happening on the surface. But beneath the ground, roots are forming, growth is taking place, and eventually, the seed will break through into the sunlight. Without the patience to wait and the persistence to nurture that seed, we might give up before it has the chance to bloom.

Similarly, many of the most significant achievements in life require us to endure through periods of seeming stagnation. Whether we're working on personal growth, a career milestone, a relationship, or a creative project, patience allows us to see the value in the journey rather than just the destination. Persistence, on the other hand, ensures that we continue to move forward, even when progress is slow.

Patience as a Foundation for Growth

Patience is more than just the ability to wait. It is an active quality that involves maintaining hope, discipline, and focus over time. Patience teaches us to trust in the process, even when the outcome is not immediately clear. Much like the white crayon, whose presence in a drawing may not be obvious at first glance but becomes essential over time, patience allows us to appreciate the long-term value of our efforts.

One of the greatest gifts of patience is that it helps us develop resilience. Life's challenges can be overwhelming, and it's easy to feel discouraged when things don't go according to plan. But when we cultivate patience, we learn to sit with discomfort, uncertainty, and setbacks without giving up. Patience allows us to weather the storms and see beyond the immediate difficulties, trusting that with time and persistence, we will find a way forward.

Consider the process of learning a new skill. At the beginning, it's common to struggle and feel frustrated. Whether we're learning to play an instrument, speak a new language, or develop a new professional competency, the early stages are often filled with mistakes and setbacks. Without patience, we might abandon our efforts prematurely. But with patience, we give ourselves the space to grow at our own pace, knowing that mastery doesn't happen overnight.

Patience also fosters a deeper sense of self-awareness. In a world that rewards quick fixes, we often miss the opportunity to reflect on our motivations, challenges, and desires. When we practice patience, we take the time to look inward, to understand our thoughts and emotions, and to make decisions that align with our values rather than our impulses. This deeper understanding of ourselves allows for more meaningful and thoughtful growth over time.

The Role of Persistence in Overcoming Obstacles

While patience helps us endure the waiting, persistence gives us the strength to keep going, even when progress feels slow or difficult. Persistence is the refusal to give up, the determination to keep working toward our goals despite setbacks, and the belief that, with time and effort, we can overcome obstacles.

The journey of the white crayon can serve as a metaphor for persistence. Initially overlooked, the white crayon might seem insignificant compared to its more vibrant counterparts. But over time, as the artist continues to create, the white crayon becomes indispensable, adding light, depth, and contrast to the image. In the same way, persistence often requires us to keep going, even when our contributions or efforts feel unseen or undervalued.

Persistence is not about pushing ourselves to exhaustion or forcing outcomes. Rather, it's about maintaining steady, consistent effort, trusting that each step we take is moving us closer to our goal. It's the understanding that progress is not always linear, and setbacks are part of the process. When we persist, we learn to embrace failure as a stepping stone to success, rather than a reason to quit.

One of the most important aspects of persistence is the ability to adapt. Persistence does not mean stubbornly sticking to a single approach. Instead, it involves being flexible and open to change, while still keeping our ultimate goal in mind. If one method isn't working, persistence encourages us to try another. If we face a roadblock, persistence motivates us to find a way around it. It's about being resourceful and creative in the face of challenges, rather than giving up when things don't go as planned.

The Long-Term Impact of Patience and Persistence

While quick wins can be satisfying in the moment, the most meaningful achievements in life often come from long-term, sustained effort. Patience and persistence allow us to build something lasting and impactful, whether it's in our personal lives, our careers, or our relationships.

Consider the stories of some of the most successful people in history — writers, artists, inventors, and entrepreneurs. Their journeys were rarely easy, and they often faced numerous failures along the way. But through patience and persistence, they continued to work toward their goals, refining their craft, learning from their mistakes, and ultimately achieving greatness.

In our own lives, the same principles apply. Whether we're striving to build a meaningful career, cultivate strong relationships, or develop new skills, patience and persistence are the keys to lasting success. These qualities remind us that the journey is just as important as the destination, and that real, meaningful progress takes time.

Conclusion: Embracing the Journey

Patience and persistence are quiet virtues, often overshadowed by the more immediate rewards of bold action and quick results. But much like the white crayon's subtle yet essential contributions to a drawing, these qualities have a profound and lasting impact on our lives. They remind us that not all progress is visible at first, and that the most meaningful achievements often require time, effort, and the willingness to endure through challenges.

By embracing patience and persistence, we cultivate resilience, adaptability, and a deeper sense of purpose. We learn to appreciate the journey, trust in the process, and keep moving forward, even when success seems far away. And in doing so, we build something lasting, something meaningful — a life shaped by steady, thoughtful progress, rather than fleeting victories.

CHAPTER 7:
THE BEAUTY OF DIVERSITY AND COLLABORATION

The white crayon, despite its unique contributions to a drawing, doesn't work in isolation. It collaborates with other colors to bring an image to life. This idea of working together — of combining different talents, perspectives, and strengths — mirrors one of the most fundamental truths in life: we are all stronger when we embrace diversity and collaborate. The white crayon's story teaches us that beauty, depth, and innovation often emerge from differences, and that diversity is not something to be tolerated, but celebrated and harnessed for collective success.

In this chapter, we'll explore how diversity and collaboration are essential for creativity, problem-solving, and building meaningful relationships. We'll examine the power of different perspectives, the richness that comes from blending unique talents, and how working together with others leads to greater achievements than any one person could accomplish alone. Much like how every color in the crayon box has its own role to play, every individual, with their distinct experiences and abilities, contributes to a vibrant and successful whole.

The Power of Different Perspectives

One of the most remarkable aspects of diversity is the way it introduces us to new perspectives. In a world where sameness often feels safe, it's tempting to surround ourselves with people who think, look, and act like us. However, the true beauty of diversity lies in the fresh ideas, alternative approaches, and unique viewpoints that others bring to the table.

Imagine a drawing made entirely with one color. It might be clear and bold, but it would also be flat and limited. Now think of a drawing where multiple colors work together — the contrast between light and dark, the interplay of warm and cool tones, the subtle blending of hues to create depth and dimension. It's this combination of colors that brings richness to the picture. In the same way, different perspectives add depth and complexity to our understanding of the world.

When we collaborate with people from different backgrounds, we open ourselves up to new ways of thinking. Diversity challenges us to question our assumptions, broaden our horizons, and approach problems from multiple angles. Whether it's in the workplace, in social settings, or in our personal lives, embracing diversity allows us to see opportunities we might have otherwise missed and come up with solutions that are more innovative and inclusive.

Consider the world of business and innovation. Many of the most groundbreaking ideas come from teams that bring together individuals with diverse skill sets, cultural backgrounds, and perspectives. By combining these different viewpoints, teams are able to think outside the box, challenge conventional wisdom, and develop products or solutions that resonate with a wider audience. Diversity fuels creativity by ensuring that no single way of thinking dominates the conversation. Instead, it encourages a flow of ideas that enriches the final outcome.

Celebrating Our Unique Strengths

Just as the crayons in a box each bring something unique to a drawing, every person brings their own set of strengths to the table. Whether these strengths are creative, analytical, emotional, or technical, they all have a place and are necessary for success. Collaboration allows us to leverage these diverse talents, creating something far greater than what any one individual could achieve on their own.

In the story of the white crayon, its unique ability to add light and clarity complements the vibrant colors of its counterparts. Without the white crayon, the drawing would lack balance, but without the other colors, the drawing would lack vibrancy. This interdependence is what makes collaboration so powerful — every contribution matters, and when combined, these contributions create something truly extraordinary.

In our own lives, it's important to recognize and celebrate our own strengths, as well as the strengths of others. We often fall into the trap of thinking that certain skills or talents are more valuable than others, but in reality, it's the diversity of these abilities that leads to success. A team made up solely of visionaries may have bold ideas, but without the practical thinkers to execute them, those ideas may never come to fruition. Similarly, a group of problem-solvers might excel at finding solutions, but without the creative thinkers to envision new possibilities, they might struggle to innovate.

Collaboration is about bringing these different strengths together in a way that complements and enhances each other. It's about recognizing that we don't have to do everything ourselves and that by working with others, we can achieve far more than we ever could alone. In this way, collaboration becomes not just a practical necessity, but a celebration of the unique gifts that each person brings to the table.

Overcoming Challenges Through Collaboration

Challenges and obstacles are an inevitable part of life, and it's in these moments that the power of collaboration truly shines. When we face difficulties on our own, it's easy to feel overwhelmed or stuck. But when we collaborate with others, we gain access to new resources, ideas, and perspectives that can help us overcome even the toughest challenges.

In the same way that a complex drawing might require the careful blending of multiple colors to create the desired effect, many problems require a collaborative effort to solve. Each person involved brings their own experience and expertise, allowing the group to tackle the issue from different angles. Collaboration turns what might seem like an insurmountable challenge into a shared endeavor, where the strengths of each individual contribute to the collective success.

Moreover, collaboration fosters resilience. When we work with others, we are not alone in our struggles. We have a support system that can offer encouragement, advice, and alternative solutions when things get tough. This sense of community and shared purpose gives us the strength to keep going, even when the road ahead is difficult.

One of the key benefits of collaboration is the ability to combine different problem-solving approaches. Some people are natural innovators, always looking for creative ways to approach challenges. Others are more methodical, focusing on step-by-step solutions. Still, others are skilled at mediating conflicts and finding common ground in disagreements. When we collaborate, we bring all of these approaches together, allowing us to find more comprehensive and effective solutions than we could on our own.

Building Meaningful Relationships

At its core, collaboration is about relationships. It's about building connections with others based on mutual respect, trust, and a shared vision. These relationships are the foundation of any successful collaboration, whether in a professional setting or in our personal lives.

The white crayon's journey reminds us that working together is not just about achieving a goal, but about the relationships we build along the way. When we collaborate with others, we develop a deeper understanding of their strengths, perspectives, and experiences. We learn to appreciate the value they bring, and in turn, they learn to appreciate us. This mutual appreciation leads to stronger, more meaningful relationships that are built on trust and respect.

Collaboration also teaches us the importance of humility. In order to work effectively with others, we must be willing to acknowledge that we don't have all the answers and that we can learn from the contributions of others. This humility fosters a sense of openness and curiosity, allowing us to grow both personally and professionally.

Conclusion: A Tapestry of Collaboration

The beauty of collaboration and diversity is that they allow us to create something greater than the sum of its parts. Just as a drawing comes to life through the interplay of different colors, our lives are enriched by the unique contributions of those around us. When we embrace diversity and work together, we unlock new possibilities, overcome challenges, and build deeper connections with others.

The lesson of the white crayon's journey is clear: no one color, no one person, can do it all. It's through collaboration that we create something truly beautiful, something that reflects the richness and complexity of the world around us. By celebrating our differences and working together, we can achieve far more than we ever could alone.

CHAPTER 8:
THE QUIET TRIUMPH OF SELF-ACCEPTANCE

The journey of the white crayon has been one of subtle growth, quiet strength, and lessons that speak to the heart of life itself. Through its story, we've learned the importance of subtlety, patience, persistence, diversity, and collaboration. Now, as the journey comes to a close, we are reminded of the most important lesson of all — the power of self-acceptance.

This final chapter focuses on the quiet but powerful triumph that comes from embracing who we are, just as the white crayon ultimately accepts its own unique value. It is a story of how realizing our worth, even when it's not immediately visible to others, can bring profound happiness, fulfillment, and purpose. The white crayon's story reflects our own paths toward self-discovery and self-acceptance, leading to a happy conclusion that motivates us to embrace our individuality and our quiet yet invaluable role in the larger picture of life.

Realizing One's Worth

For much of its journey, the white crayon felt unseen and underappreciated, overshadowed by the brighter and bolder colors in the box. It questioned its place in the artist's hand and wondered if it had any value at all. This doubt and insecurity reflect the struggles we all face at times, especially in a world that often rewards the loudest voices and the most visible contributions. We may feel like we don't stand out enough, or that our quiet qualities go unnoticed.

However, the turning point in the white crayon's story — and in our own — comes when it begins to understand that its worth lies not in being the brightest, but in being essential in its own way. When the artist reaches for the white crayon to add light to dark areas, to create balance in the picture, and to add the finishing touches that bring the whole drawing to life, the crayon realizes that its role is not less important, but different. Its subtle, quiet impact is necessary for the drawing to be complete.

This realization is a powerful moment of self-acceptance. The white crayon no longer seeks to be like the other colors, nor does it diminish its own importance. Instead, it embraces its unique contribution to the picture, understanding that without it, the drawing would lack depth and harmony. This acceptance brings the white crayon peace and a sense of belonging — not because it has changed, but because it has finally recognized the value of who it has always been.

The Joy of Being True to Oneself

Self-acceptance is not just about acknowledging our strengths; it's about finding joy in being exactly who we are. For the white crayon, this means recognizing that its quiet contributions — though not always obvious or celebrated — are deeply meaningful. In the same way, when we accept ourselves, we stop comparing ourselves to others and start celebrating our own unique gifts.

The joy of self-acceptance is transformative. It allows us to feel comfortable in our own skin, to trust our own path, and to contribute to the world in ways that feel authentic to us. Just as the white crayon finds its place in the artist's hand, we, too, find our place in the world when we embrace who we are without hesitation or doubt. This self-assurance allows us to move forward with confidence and peace, knowing that we don't have to be anyone else but ourselves to make a meaningful impact.

Completing the Picture

In the end, the white crayon's role is fully realized when the drawing is complete. Every color has played its part, and the white crayon's subtle highlights bring light and clarity to the final image. The drawing is beautiful not just because of the bold strokes of color, but because of the balance and harmony that the white crayon helps create. The artist smiles, knowing that each crayon was essential in bringing the vision to life.

This moment of completion mirrors the way we contribute to the world around us. Each of us, with our different talents, perspectives, and strengths, plays a part in the larger picture. When we embrace our own role — whether it's bold and visible, or quiet and behind the scenes — we help create something that is greater than the sum of its parts. Just like the white crayon, we are all essential to the overall beauty and balance of life.

A Happy and Motivated Closure

As the white crayon's story comes to a close, we are left with a powerful sense of motivation and fulfillment. The crayon, once overlooked and unsure of its place, has discovered its true worth and embraced its role with confidence and joy. It no longer seeks validation from others, because it has found peace in knowing its own value.

The message of the white crayon's journey is clear: true happiness and fulfillment come not from external recognition, but from within. By accepting ourselves, we unlock our full potential and find contentment in being exactly who we are. The white crayon's quiet triumph reminds us that we don't have to be the loudest, the brightest, or the most visible to make a difference.

Sometimes, it's our subtle, quiet contributions that have the most lasting and meaningful impact.

Conclusion: The Lasting Impact of Self-Acceptance

The story of the white crayon teaches us that every individual has a role to play, and every contribution matters. Just as the drawing would be incomplete without the white crayon's light and balance, the world would be incomplete without the unique gifts that each of us brings. The happy ending of the white crayon's journey is not just about finding its place in the drawing, but about realizing that it has always been valuable, just as it is.

As we close this chapter, we are reminded that self-acceptance is the key to a fulfilled and motivated life. By embracing who we are, we unlock the power to contribute meaningfully to the world, to find joy in our own journey, and to create a life that is both impactful and true to ourselves.

www.ingramcontent.com/pod-product-compliance
Lightning Source LLC
LaVergne TN
LVHW041549070526
838199LV00046B/1885